Short Walks from
Ambleside and Grasmere

The Lake District National Park

The Lake District National Park is the biggest of England's National Parks. Its 885 square mile area is best loved for the variety and contrast of its landscape. Here you can see high fells, rocky crags, lush green dales with long still lakes, vibrant villages and quiet hamlets. You can also see England's highest mountain (Scafell Pike) and her deepest lake (Wastwater), as well as investigating the history of literary legends such as Wordsworth.

The Lake District National Park is a celebration of how people and nature can work together. Although the Lake District countryside may seem wild, it looks the way it does because of human activity, particularly farming. People have been using the area for at least 10,000 years and in 1951 it was established as a National Park to protect it for future generations.

The land of the Lake District National Park is nearly all privately owned and much of it farmed. Because of this it is especially important that you use the Country Code to guide your activities in the National Park.

Short Walks from Ambleside and Grasmere

Paul Buttle

Published by
amadorn

I would like to express here my thanks
to Ian Robinson who provided the ideas for
three of the walks in this guide

ISBN 0 9519345 7 0
First published March 2002. Reprinted April 2003.

Published by Amadorn, 18 Brewery Lane, Keswick, Cumbria.
Typeset by Ferguson Bros. (Printers) Ltd., Keswick, Cumbria.
Maps by Gelder, Much Dewchurch, Herefordshire.
Printed by Nuffield Press, Abingdon, Oxfordshire

CONTENTS

INTRODUCTION

Many and beautiful are the walks about Ambleside: walks within a reasonable distance for any fair pedestrian, and which all but very fine ladies, or very delicate ones, may take without too much fatigue, and without risk or danger if they are moderately careful.

These words were written by Eliza Lynn Linton in 1864. I came across them when I had all but completed preparing this guide. It struck me that Eliza Lynn no doubt had in mind when she wrote those words many of the walks I had decided should go in this guide. Making allowance for her Victorian sensibilities she described pretty well the sort of walks I set out to include - walks not overtaxing, nor hazardous yet still very enjoyable - short walks in the sense that they need very little time to accomplish as they demand very little effort.

Timing of walks

Each walk has a suggested time but this should be regarded simply as a rule of thumb. I've tended to give, I think, a fairly generous time allowances for each walk but some users may not think so. The times I have given do not allow for any stops either. So where I have suggested a walk takes only two hours to do, dawdling, picnicking and stopping to admire the scenery could easily mean it could take up the whole afternoon.

Order of walks

On first examination it may not seem that there is any logic to the way the walks in this guide are ordered, but there is - they are ordered roughly according to the effort involved in completing them. Thus the easiest walk comes first and the hardest last.

Which map to use?

It may well be possible to do all the walks simply relying on the directional notes and sketch maps provided, however, it is always best to have a map. There are three Ordnance Survey Maps which can be used with this guide:

Outdoor Leisure 4 - English Lakes South Eastern. Scale 1:25,000

This is an incredibly detailed map and covers all the walks described in this guide except for the Mickleden walk. Because of its representation of field boundaries it is the best map to have on low level walks.

The "One Inch" Tourist Map of the Lake District. Scale 1: 63,360.

This map covers all the walks in this guide and much more besides, unfortunately it is now out of print but it is still well worth getting hold of a second hand copy if you can.

Landranger Series Sheet 90. Scale 1:50,000

Like the "One Inch" it covers all the walks in this guide. Although only a slightly larger scale than the "One Inch" map it is surprisingly clearer.

What else to take

The highest point reached on any of the walks in this guide is about 1,200 feet on the Alcock Tarn walk, even so given how the weather can change in the Lake District the following items will be of advantage - unless it is a really hot day: a waterproof or windproof outer jacket, sturdy boots with a good sole pattern, hat and gloves and spare warm clothing, a comfortable day sack, food and something to drink. And to be really safe if you go above 1000 feet: a compass, torch and whistle. To check on Lake District weather conditions phone 017687 75757.

And if it should rain...?

One of my great pleasures whilst preparing this guide has been to visit the Armit Library in Ambleside. It is a treasure house of local history, reference books and literary sources beautifully housed and furnished. Any walker based in Ambleside and interested in history or literature and knowing the existence of this library will surely find themselves torn betwixt wishing for fine weather the better to enjoy a day out on the hill, and wishing for a deluge which will give them an excuse to ensconce themselves happily in this library for the day.

I began this introduction with a quote from Eliza Lynn Linton's book "The Lake Country" I will close with another simply because it is such a wonderful quote though I own it has no real relevance to this introduction - but it deserves to be much better known. It appears as a footnote on page 31 of her book.

> *In a few years.....pretty, dirty, neglected Troutbeck will be cleaned, schooled, and ornamented, and made fit company for ambitious Windermere and respectable Ambleside. It is worth seeing, however, in its dirt and neglect; its tumbledown cottages - not one among them all straight according to the plumb line - with ivied walls and casements patched with rags and paper.....its destitution and penury all so grandly enframed that its very poverty becomes a charm the more. It is one of the real bye-hamlets of the lake district, picturesque, wild, dirty and diseased, which the prosaic architect and schoolmaster will sweep away before many years are gone.*

How very perspicacious Miss E. L. Linton was.

March 2002

Mickleden

Distance	2 miles
Total feet of climbing	Negligible
Suggested time	1 hour
Starting point	Old Dungeon Ghyll car park (NY 284 060)
Public transport	Bus service 516 see page 36

This is a very easy, almost level, walk which yet has a great feeling of venturing into the wilderness about it as it approaches some of the most rugged fells in the Lake District: Crinkle Crags, Rossett Pike and Bowfell. Overlooking Mickleden to the north is the striking peak of Pike of Stickle that sticks out like a proverbial sore thumb. As the information box on the opposite page explains this peak, long ago, was once a site of great industry. Gazing up at Pike of Stickle and pondering on what an important place this once was to our ancestors is very thought provoking.

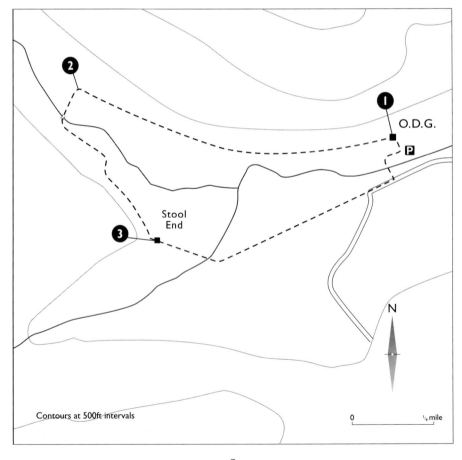

O.D.G.

Stool End

Contours at 500ft intervals

N

0   ¹⁄₄ mile

1 From the Old Dungeon Ghyll car park follow the driveway that leads round the eastern gable end of the public bar of the hotel. Where the driveway turns sharp right towards a stone cottage continue straight forward on a stony path leading to a five bar gate next to which is also a kissing gate. Within a few yards of passing through either of these gates a National Trust sign indicates that the path leads to Mickleden. The path follows the course of a stone wall until it takes a sharp left hand turn at which point the valley is completely open and unenclosed. ($^3/_4$ mile)

The Mickleden path offers at this point another three quarters of a mile of easy level walking before dividing into two steep Lakeland paths. Moving along this path away from houses, roads and fields the sense of being in a wilderness increases. Users of this guide may, therefore, like to investigate this section of the valley before following the next directional note.

2 Here turn left following the altered course of the wall. There is a path but being very little used it is not immediately obvious, however, in the space of a few hundred yards you come to Mickleden Beck and a broad wooden footbridge. The path leading from the other side of the bridge, initially following the beck downstream, is very evident. This is a permitted path which leads to Stool End Farm. Where the path comes to a gate with the word "Private" on it simply bear right and then left to a second gate which is the correct one to pass through. ($^1/_2$ mile)

3 From Stool End Farm follow the farm's access road back to the public road. Follow the road some eighty yards eastwards and turn left on to the short surfaced lane leading to the Old Dungeon Ghyll car park and the start of the walk. ($^3/_4$ mile)

Langdale Stone Axe Factory

In October 1947 a Mr Brian Bunch from Leamington Spa on a climbing holiday with his wife in Langdale, but frustrated by bad weather, decided to explore Pike of Stickle. In so doing he discovered the site of the largest neolithic stone axe factory in England which had seemingly lain undisturbed for over four thousand years after being exploited for perhaps a thousand years. The exceptional flint-like, rather than slate-like, quality of the rock in this area made it possible for neolithic man to shape the scree fragments he found there into axe heads which he then most probably took to the coast in order to have them more finely shaped and polished with sandstone. Langdale stone axes have been found in Scotland, the Isle of Man and as far south as Dorset. The site has been so rifled since its discovery, however, it is unlikely there are any more finds to be made - but hundreds of rejected axes were discovered here, an example of which, together with a finished polished version, can be seen in the Armit Museum in Ambleside.

Stock Ghyll

Distance	2 miles
Total feet of climbing	400 feet
Suggested time	1 hour
Starting point	Ambleside (NY 377 045)

Stock Ghyll is as dramatic a waterfall as one will see anywhere in the Lake District. Though only half a mile from the centre of Ambleside there must be many thousands who visit the town who have no idea of its existence, for it takes a little investigation to find. Whilst many will view the waterfall and then return to the bustle of Ambleside this walk continues further along the course of Stock Ghyll to view the valley which it forms. The return route passes through a hamlet called Seathwaite, the least known of the three Seathwaites which are located in Cumbria and which formerly were in three separate counties.

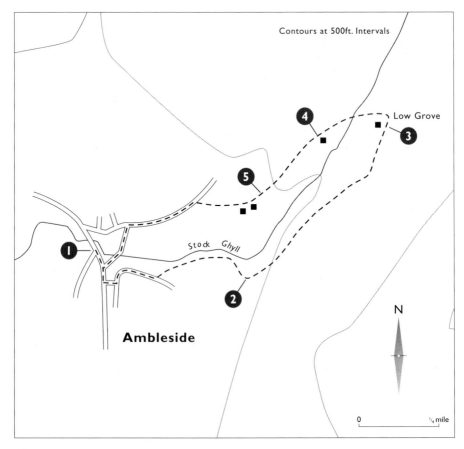

Contours at 500ft. Intervals

Low Grove

Stock Ghyll

N

Ambleside

0   ¼ mile

1 From the centre of Ambleside walk southwards to Barclays Bank. Here turn left in to the lane, Stock Ghyll Lane, that runs between the bank and the Market Hall. The lane makes a sharp left hand turn at the back of the bank and starts climbing uphill. Roughly 400 yards along this road a large sign with the words "This way to the waterfalls" points to a broad path leading off to the left. The path is waymarked with some distinctive red arrows. Follow these waymarks until you come to a picnic table near which is a sign with the words "To revolving gate exit" which indicates a path leading off to the right. Follow this new path which within a hundred yards or so leads to a narrow surfaced lane. ($^1/_2$ mile)

2 Here turn left. You soon cross a cattle grid, then a second and then a third just past Low Grove House. (Note: This third cattle grid is now obviously redundant and could easily be removed whilst this guide still remains in print!) Immediately after crossing the third cattle grid is a waymarked trackway leading off to the left. ($^1/_2$ mile)

3 The trackway almost immediately branches in two. Take the left hand, more distinct trackway, which leads down to a wooden bridge spanning Stock Ghyll. From the bridge a path follows the course of the beck a few score yards and then loops back on itself. At the apex of this loop scrutinise the wall to the left of you to locate a none too obvious stone stile. Climbing over the stile is a little difficult as it also involves stepping over a small beck at the same time. Once over head for a small barn about one hundred yards ahead. ($^1/_4$ mile)

4 Next to the barn is a six bar gate and kissing gate. Here you join a very grassy trackway which a few hundred yards on passes through another paired gate and kissing gate and then swings left through another gateway. At the point the trackway swings left, however, the right of way continues directly forward, downhill, along the side of the stone wall ahead of you towards a stone built dwelling where one passes through two more gateways to gain access to the terminus of a surfaced access road. ($^1/_4$ mile)

5 Follow the access road downhill through the hamlet of Seathwaite to its junction with the Kirkstone Road. Here turn left. Follow the road roughly three hundred yards downhill and then turn left, just past the entrance to the Kirkstone Foot holiday cottages, in to Fairview Road which in turn leads to Peggy Hill which brings you directly back to Ambleside's Market Cross. ($^1/_2$ mile)

The two walks presented on this page and the next can obviously be combined together to form a circular walk, however, the combined distance then involved is five and a half miles and as this is intended to be a guide to short walks I have decided to present them as two separate walks leaving it up to the user to chose whether to combine them or not. If treated as separate walks the two frequent buses services along the A591 make it easy to return to whichever starting point is chosen. While there are a number of car parks in Grasmere parking in Rydal is limited to roadside parking on the road leading up to Rydal Mount.

Rydal to Grasmere

Distance	2 miles
Total feet of climbing	200 feet
Suggested time	1 hour
Starting point	Rydal (NY 365 062)
Public transport	Bus services 555 and 599 see page 36

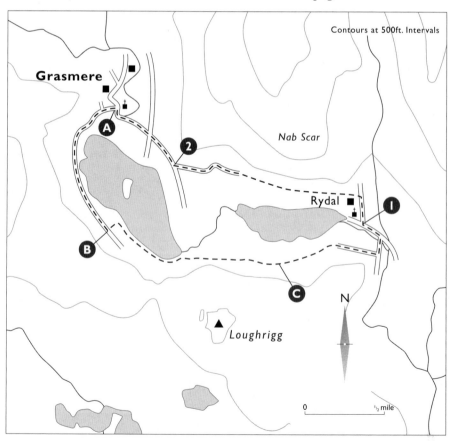

This walk uses a very pleasing old bridleway that connects Rydal to Grasmere, passing two of Wordsworth's homes: Rydal Mount, where he lived almost half his lifetime, and Dove Cottage, both open to the public.

1   From the main road in Rydal follow the road opposite Rydal Lodge leading uphill and signposted as leading to Rydal Hall, Rydal Church and Rydal Mount. Immediately after passing Rydal Mount turn left on to a trackway which passes the gable end of Rydal Mount and is signposted as being a public bridleway to Grasmere. Eventually, a little surprisingly, the bridleway becomes surfaced and gradually widens to become a roadway, soon after which it comes to a road junction. (1½ miles)

2   Here turn right and follow the road downhill past Dove Cottage and across the main A591, where it becomes Stock Lane, into the village of Grasmere. (½ mile)

Grasmere to Rydal

Distance	3¼ miles
Total feet of climbing	200 feet
Suggested time	1½ hours
Starting point	Grasmere (NY 328 047)
Public transport	Bus services 555 and 599 see page 36

This is firstly a lakeside walk along Grasmere followed by a more elevated walk, Loughrigg Terrace, above Rydal Water. On the northern shore of Rydal Water is Nab Cottage where once lived a Miss Peggy Simpson whom Thomas De Quincey visited assiduously for a number of years and finally married in 1817 three months after she bore him a son.

A   From the bridge spanning the River Rothay in the centre of Grasmere walk a few yards past St. Oswald's Church and turn left on to the road signposted as leading to the Information Centre. Follow this road for almost a mile till you locate a six bar gate on your left, over which is a fine view of Grasmere lake. Sited in the left hand wall leading to the gate is a narrow gated gap giving access to a small flight of wooden steps which is the start of a permissive lake shore path. (¾ mile)

B   Continue along this path and on reaching the outflow of the lake, about forty yards before reaching the rather sturdy footbridge that crosses it, follow the small path that veers off to the right. After breasting the crest of a short ridge the path divides in two. Keep to the right hand branch, the higher one, traversing the lower slopes of Loughrigg above Rydal Water. This path reaches quite a spectacular 'cavern', the result of past quarrying, which is well worth some exploration. (1½ miles)

C   From the 'cavern' the path descends to the left and becomes a trackway that upgrades to a surfaced roadway when reaching a group of cottages. Within another quarter of a mile the road comes to a junction. Here turn left to join the main A591, upon reaching which turn left once more. The walk's starting point is now only a few hundred yards further on. (1 mile)

The Rydal Round

Distance	3¹/₄ miles
Total feet of climbing	100 feet
Suggested time	1¹/₂ hours
Starting point	Ambleside (NY 377 045)

This walk is basically an easy, almost level, saunter round the Rothay valley between Ambleside and the hamlet of Rydal. Though the return route is mostly by road it is a road that has very few cars using it for which there is a simple explanation - in theory it is closed to general traffic. Unfortunately this injunction is not always observed but even so the road is very quiet compared to other Lakeland lanes and gives some impression of what it was once like to walk along a country lane free of cars.

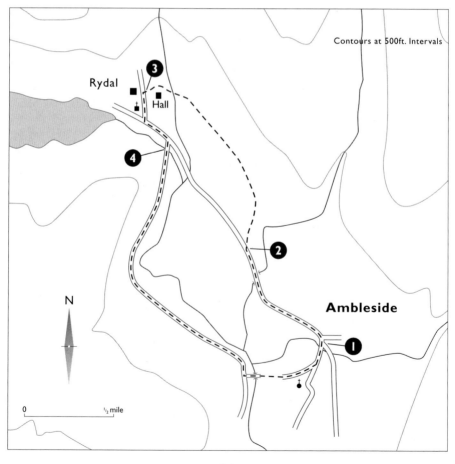

1 From the Market Cross follow the main road through Ambleside northwards towards Grasmere using the pavement on the left hand side of the road. About fifty yards after crossing a road bridge which spans Scandale Beck cross over the road to stand in front of two large ornate metal gates which stand at the entrance to a long unsurfaced driveway. ($\frac{1}{2}$ mile).

2 To the right hand side of the gates is a much smaller gate which gives access to the driveway if the main gates are locked. Though very private looking, as a signpost next to the bus stop you pass to reach the gates indicates, the driveway is actually a public right of way to Rydal Hall. The trackway eventually branches in two. Here you should bear right, as a footpath sign indicates, towards some outbuildings of Rydal Hall. This branch of the trackway leads round the back of the hall and eventually comes to a surfaced roadway. (1 mile)

3 Here turn left. Within a few hundred yards the road comes the main A591. Cross the main road to use the pathway on the other side and turn left. Within a few hundred yards turn sharp right over a humpbacked bridge spanning the River Rothay on to a narrow surfaced roadway which immediately branches in two. ($\frac{1}{4}$ mile)

4 Follow the left hand branch. After walking slightly more than a mile, and immediately after crossing a cattle grid, leading off to the left over a stone footbridge is an unsigned footpath leading to Ambleside's Rothay Park. Once over the bridge bear right on to a surfaced pathway which leads through Rothay Park to a roadway which leads to the centre of Ambleside. ($1\frac{1}{2}$ miles)

Rydal Hall and Rydal Mount

Rydal Hall was the home of the Le Fleming family from 1595 to 1970. Originally a modest farmhouse it was developed into one of the major houses in the Lake District. In 1799 it had just been newly enlarged and painted when Coleridge and Wordsworth took a walk past the front of it. They were reproved for doing so by one of the servants - a trespass which Coleridge thought was roughly equal "with the Trespass on the Eye by his damned White washing!" In 1970 the Hall was purchased by the diocese of Carlisle, after having leased it the previous seven years, and is now used as a conference and retreat centre.

Rydal Mount was the home of Wordsworth from 1813 until his death in 1850. During this period he was visited by several other poets, including: Keats in 1818 who found Wordsworth was out for the day; Tennyson in 1835 who thought of Rydal Mount "Never was a poet more comfortably housed"; and the twelve year old Algernon Charles Swinburne in 1849 to whom Wordsworth read Gray's Elegy - and which Swinburne hated ever after.

Great Langdale

Distance	3 ¼ miles
Total feet of climbing	200 feet
Suggested time	1½ hours
Starting point	Elterwater car park. (NY 328 047)
Public transport	Bus service 516 see page 36

This is a short circular walk around the eastern end of Great Langdale following the course of Great Langdale Beck outwards and using a more wooded route on the return journey. On the outward journey there are inspiring views of the Langdale Pikes, perhaps the most dramatic looking group of peaks in the Lake District. With no steep gradients to tackle this is an easy saunter - even so it still provides sufficient exercise to make the pleasures and comforts of the Britannia Inn in Elterwater better appreciated than would otherwise be the case.

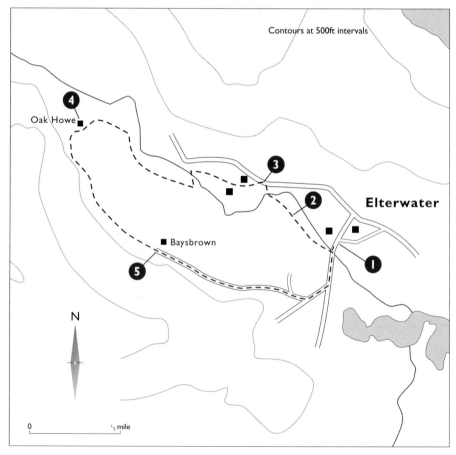

1 From the centre of Elterwater follow the road signposted as leading to Coniston and Little Langdale. Immediately after crossing the river which runs through the village turn right on to a surfaced lane which is signposted as being a cul-de-sac. Some four hundred yards along this lane the word "Footpath" on a large block of stone points to a pathway which branches off to the right. (¼ mile)

2 The pathway runs closer to the river's edge and within a few hundred yards comes to a wooden footbridge spanning the river. Cross over the bridge to join the main Langdale road on the other side of the river. Here turn left. Within about one hundred yards along this road branch left on to a stony trackway signposted as being a public footpath. (¼ mile)

3 Within a few hundred yards the trackway comes to a surfaced lane, an access road to Thrang Farm and Thrang Garth. Here turn left. On reaching Thrang Garth the right of way continues as an unsurfaced trackway round the gable end of Thrang Garth and within a hundred yards or so links up to a much broader trackway. Here turn left. Within a few hundred yards the trackway crosses a stone bridge spanning Great Langdale Beck and then follows the course of the river upstream, eventually arriving at an isolated dwelling called Oak Howe. (1 mile)

4 Here the right of way continues as a pathway which leads round the back of the large barn which stands behind the domicile. At the rear of the barn the path branches in two. Take the left hand branch which loops back down the valley. By degrees the path broadens into a trackway which eventually reaches Baysbrown Farm. (¾ mile)

5 Here the trackway continues as a surfaced lane which serves as an access road to the farm. The lane eventually joins the Coniston to Elterwater road. Here turn left to return to Elterwater and the start of the walk. (1 mile)

The Elterwater Gunpowder Company

At the start of this walk looking across the river one cannot fail to notice a large holiday development - the Langdale Timeshare Estate. The complex is built on the site of a former gunpowder mill. Taking advantage of the local availability of water power and charcoal, gunpowder was manufactured on this site from 1824 to 1928. In the early part of the last century the Elterwater Gunpowder Company employed 70 to 80 hands - both men and women. The industry was responsible for much of the present look of Elterwater today - including the workers' cottages and the bowling green which was provided by the company in 1910 for the benefit of their workers and local inhabitants alike.

The Troutbeck Round

Distance	3 ¼ miles
Total feet of climbing	600 feet
Suggested time	1½ hours
Starting point	Troutbeck (NY 411 035)
Public transport	Bus service 108A see page 36

Troutbeck is one of the more interesting and appealing villages in the Lake District. It has an unusual situation and layout strung along the western slopes of the valley it occupies giving every house a commanding view of the dale. This walk follows a route round the spur of fell-land that rises above the village mostly by way of enclosed trackways. On the outward journey there are views of lake Windermere. But the best views are perhaps those obtained on reaching the highest part of the walk when there comes in to view the even higher peaks of Ill Bell and Froswick.

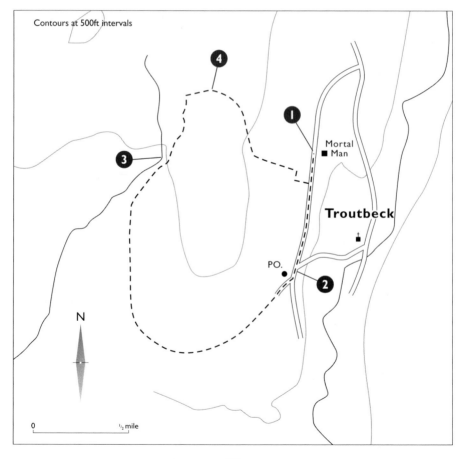

Contours at 500ft intervals

4

1

Mortal
■ Man

3

Troutbeck

PO.

2

N

0   ½ mile

1 Beginning from the Mortal Man's inn sign walk in a southerly direction on the main road through the village. On reaching the village post office, sited in the ground floor of the village institute, bear right past the village institute's flag pole on to a signposted public bridleway: Robin Lane. ($^1\!/_2$ mile)

2 After a distance of three quarters of a mile the lane becomes gated. At this point branching off to the left through another gateway is a signposted bridleway to Skelghyll. Ignore this bridleway and continue on the lane which now becomes Hundreds Road. Passing through a final gate the trackway becomes unenclosed and loops round to the left over a small stone bridge. ($1^1\!/_2$ miles)

3 Just before crossing the bridge leading off to the right is a signposted path to Wansfell and Nanny Lane. The path is waymarked with small wooden posts on which are fixed round signs bearing a white arrow. The path eventually links up to a much broader path leading down from the top of Wansfell at a point where it passes through a metal gate. Here turn right and follow the more prominent path downhill. Within a few hundred yards the path joins an enclosed trackway: Nanny Lane. ($^1\!/_2$ mile)

4 Here turn right and follow Nanny Lane downhill to Troutbeck. On reaching the roadway turn left. The Mortal Man is a hundred and fifty yards further on. ($^3\!/_4$ mile)

The Mortal Man

This inn was originally called the White House but around 1800 a local painter and patron of the inn called Julius Caesar Ibbetson painted a new sign for it. It depicted the portraits of two of his neighbours, one was a jolly fat fellow, called Nat Fleming; the other long, lean and pale, was called Ned Partridge. Beneath them was written this rhyming dialogue:-

Oh Mortal Man that lives by bread
What is it makes thy nose so red?

Thou silly fool that looks so pale
'Tis drinking Sally Birkett's ale.

The sign was such a success the inn was soon known as the Mortal Man. The original sign, however, was retained by the landlord of the inn when he retired and has since been lost. The present sign is a recreation. More regrettable still is a recent decision to introduce muzak into this venerable establishment, an imposition which Julius Caesar Ibbetson certainly did not have to endure - if he had the inn might well still be called the White House.

Ambleside to Skelwith Bridge

Distance	2 ³/₄ miles
Total feet of climbing	600 feet
Suggested time	1 ³/₄ hours
Starting point	Ambleside (NY 377 045)
Public transport	Bus services 506 and 516 see page 36

This is a linear walk which depends on using local bus services to return to the starting point. It is a pleasing ramble across the southern fringes of Loughrigg Fell offering spectacular views down the length of lake Windermere and excellent views also of the Langdale Pikes. At the walk's conclusion there is the Skelwith Bridge Hotel which serves teas, the adjacent Talbot Bar which also serves bar meals and the Kirkstone Galleries which has a surprising range of goods on display and also has a pleasant café to eat in. All places one can happily take advantage of if there is some time to wait for an omnibus.

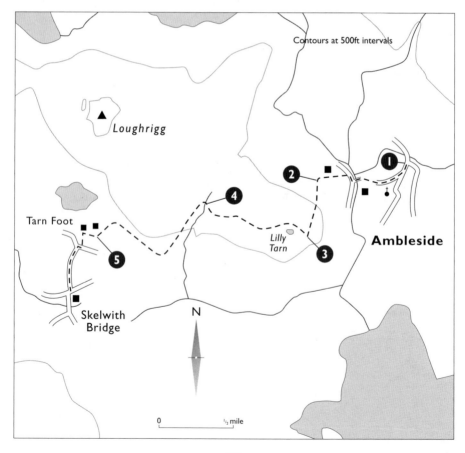

1 From the Market Cross walk downhill and turn first left in to Compston Road. At Zefferelli's cinema turn right in to Vicarage Road. The road is a cul-de-sac at the end of which a broad surfaced pathway leads through Rothay Park to a stone footbridge which spans the Rothay River giving access to a roadway. Here turn right. Fifty yards along this road turn left on to a trackway signposted as being a public bridleway. The trackway zig-zags steeply uphill. Sixty yards after passing High Barn a distinct metal public footpath sign points to a pathway leading off to the left to Clappersgate. ($\frac{1}{2}$ mile)

2 Some eighty yards after passing through a "squeeze gate" the path branches in two. Take the right hand branch. Within another hundred yards this path also branches in two. Here take the left hand branch which after a few hundred feet of ascent also bifurcates. Though it happens that these two paths merge back together the right hand branch is the better one to take. Eventually the path comes to a ladder stile spanning a stone wall. It then ascends a rocky knoll and then goes on to ascend a second rocky knoll within a further hundred yards. ($\frac{1}{4}$ mile)

3 Passing over the second knoll turn right away from the lake on to a path which leads towards the heart of Loughrigg Fell. Within a few hundred yards the path passes a small tarnlet and then a more substantial piece of water known as Lilly Tarn complete with a small islet. Continue round the right hand side of the tarn. Where the path branches in two, a few hundred yards from the tarn, take the left hand branch. Within a few hundred yards the path comes to parallel a stone wall which it then follows until it reaches a swift flowing stream. ($\frac{3}{4}$ mile)

4 Here, after crossing the stream, the path veers away from the wall and within fifty yards joins a broad bridleway. Here turn left to follow the bridleway downhill. The bridleway soon follows the line of the wall you have but recently abandoned. Following the line of this wall the bridleway eventually comes to a small hamlet called Tarn Foot. ($\frac{3}{4}$ mile)

5 Here the bridleway crosses a broad trackway leading to Loughrigg Tarn and passes round the gable end of a two storey house and then a row of cottages and comes to a surfaced access road. Here turn left. Within sixty yards the access lane joins the public highway. Here turn right and within another sixty yards turn left on to a road which leads to the main A593 at Skelwith Bridge. Immediately to the left of this junction is a bus shelter for the bus back to Ambleside. ($\frac{1}{2}$ mile)

High Sweden Bridge

Distance	2³/₄ miles
Total feet of climbing	700 feet
Suggested time	1³/₄ hours
Starting point	Ambleside (NY 377 045)

This is a steep walk at first through the streets of Ambleside, all bustle to begin with, until one passes through a six bar gate; then it almost seems as though one has stepped in to another world as one follows a rough trackway leading through a pleasant wooded valley. After crossing High Sweden Bridge there is a little more climbing up to the ridge bounding the western side of the valley and the route then turns back to Ambleside. At this point one becomes aware of the height obtained - ahead is a surprisingly panoramic view of Ambleside and Windermere lake and to the west a very pleasing view of the Rothay valley.

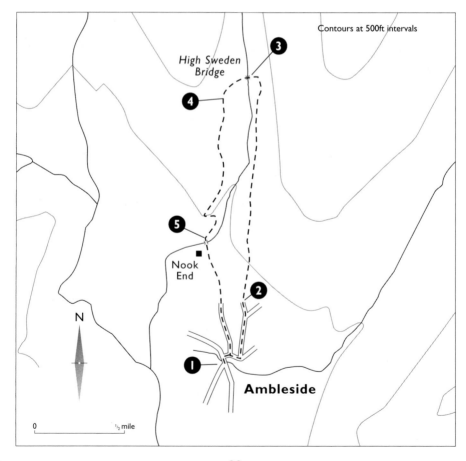

1 From the Market Cross walk in the direction of Grasmere, past Bridge House, and take the first turn right in to Smithy Brow. Swinging left this becomes the Kirkstone Road. Some fifty yards after swinging left turn left in to Sweden Bridge Lane. A hundred yards or so along the lane is Belle View Lane - be sure to ignore it. After pulling uphill three hundred yards or so the lane appears to branch in two: Sweden Bridge Lane, however, is clearly indicated as being the left hand branch. Another hundred yards on the lane comes to a six bar gate. ($\frac{1}{4}$ mile)

2 Passing through the gate Sweden Bridge Lane becomes a rough unsurfaced trackway. Eventually there comes in to view High Sweden Bridge, a parapet-less bridge spanning Scandale Beck. (1 mile)

(The trackway you have so far followed continues up the valley to Scandale Pass. Over the next mile and a quarter, however, though quite undulating, it gains little height and only starts to climb higher on reaching a large sheepfold. The valley in its upper reaches becomes quite spacious and contains a surprising number of stone walls - indeed, the trackway for much of this distance is bounded on either side with a stone wall. In short, it is well worth walking to the head of the valley to see what there is to see - though to do so, to the sheepfold and back, will add another two and a half miles to the walk.)

3 Passing through the gate on the other side of the bridge turn left. The path quickly branches in two. Follow the right hand branch which follows the line of a stone wall to a ladder stile. Two paths emanate from the ladder stile on the other side of the wall it spans. Take the left hand path which links up to another pathway at a point where it passes through a currently gateless gap in a wall which is spanned by a redundant ladder stile. ($\frac{1}{4}$ mile)

4 Turn left. This broader path winds its way down the fell towards Ambleside eventually reaching Low Sweden Bridge, by which stage it has taken on the quality of a trackway. ($\frac{3}{4}$ mile)

5 Fifty yards from the bridge the trackway enters Nook End Farm. Continue along the access lane which leads to the farm - Nook Lane. The lane leads back to Smithy Brow and the start of the walk. ($\frac{1}{2}$ mile)

Sweden Bridge acquired its name from the nearby Sweden Crag. The word Sweden in this instance is derived from an old Norse word Svíthinn meaning land cleared by burning

Loughrigg Tarn

Distance	3 ³/₄ miles
Total feet of climbing	300 feet
Suggested time	1³/₄ hours
Starting point	Elterwater car park. (NY 328 047)
Public transport	Bus service 516 see page 36

This short circuit starts with a river and lake side walk from Elterwater to Skelwith Bridge, from which point a short ascent then soon brings one to the tranquillity of Loughrigg Tarn, which has one of the most scenic settings of any tarn in the Lake District. From the tarn the walk then continues across the lower slopes of Loughrigg fell. It then follows a brief wander through the grounds of a previously grand Victorian residence, now a Youth Hostel, bringing one to a final descent across open land with fine views of the Langdale Pikes.

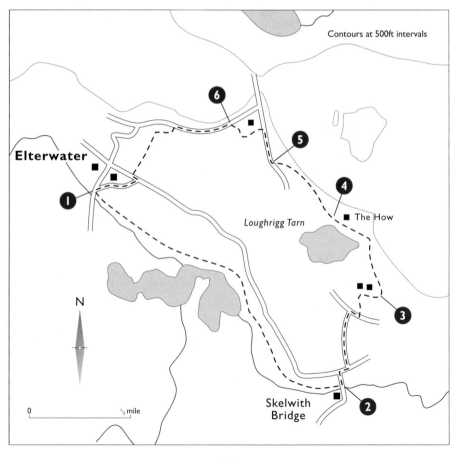

1 From the centre of Elterwater follow the road signposted as leading to Coniston. Within 50 yards turn left in to the village car park. At the far end of the car park a gate gives access to a path following the course of Great Langdale Beck. This popular path leads directly to Skelwith Bridge following first Great Langdale Beck, then the shore line of Elterwater and then the lake's outflow, the River Brathay. In its final stage it passes through a slate craft work yard to reach the main A593. (1½ miles)

2 Here turn left. Within 150 yards turn left on to an unsignposted road which runs uphill past a bus shelter and a row of four cottages. After a short climb the road comes to a junction. Here turn right. Within sixty yards on the left hand side is the start of a surfaced driveway leading up to a row of cottages. On reaching the cottages turn right on to an unsurfaced trackway that leads past the cottages and is signposted as being: "Footpath to Tarn". Within another hundred yards the track comes to another trackway. Here turn left. Almost immediately the trackway branches in two. Take the left hand branch which leads to a substantial six bar gate bearing a sign which indicates the trackway leads to Loughrigg Tarn. (½ mile)

3 The track passes round the northern side of of Loughrigg Tarn. Overlooking the tarn are two attractive cottages collectively called The How. Roughly a hundred yards beyond the furthest cottage on the right hand side of the track is a simple wooden bench bearing the inscription: "1893 R. S. 1982". (¼ mile)

4 From the bench an unsigned path leads uphill to a five bar gate. Once through the gate turn left to follow a very obvious pathway that mostly follows the wall bounding the open fell. The path eventually comes to a roadway by way of a wooden stile which crosses a metal fence. (½ mile)

5 On reaching the road turn right. Within four hundred yards on the left hand side of the road is located a long six bar gate bearing a National Trust sign with the words: "High Close Garden", which has a smaller wicket gate beside it. Pass through the smaller gate and continue on the broad gravelled pathway it gives access to. The path snakes through the grounds of High Close, now a youth hostel, broadening to a trackway on the way and eventually emerging on to another roadway. (¼ mile)

6 Here turn left. Follow the road about four hundred yards to a point where it starts to cross some open fell land. At this point branch left on to a trackway that passes a wooden bench. The track would seem to be the original roadway and soon links back up with the new roadway. Roughly one hundred yards before rejoining the new road is the start of a pathway which leads downhill towards Elterwater. On reaching the road turn left and within the space of thirty yards branch right on to a roadway leading in to Elterwater village. (¾ mile)

Alcock Tarn

Distance	2 ½ miles
Total feet of climbing	1000 feet
Suggested time	2 hours
Starting point	Grasmere (NY 328 047)
Public transport	Bus services 555 and 599 see page 36

This is by far the steepest and highest walk in the guide and whilst it is clear from the walk's title what the object is, its final revelation may yet still come as something of a surprise on what otherwise seems a very steep sided fell. Although this walk reaches only very modest heights by Lake District standards - less than 1,300 feet - nonetheless a great sense of elevation is obtained and there are to be enjoyed some very impressive vistas of Windermere and the Coniston fells and most particularly some very airy views of the vale of Grasmere itself.

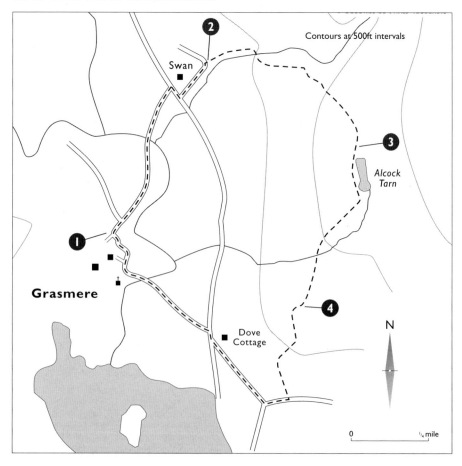

1 From the village green in Grasmere follow the road called Broadgate leading north out of the village past a red phone box. On reaching the main A591 cross over the road and continue along a lane leading past the gable end of the Swan Hotel. Some two hundred yards along this road leading off to the right is a signposted public footpath leading to Greenhead Gill and Alcock Tarn. (½ mile)

2 Initially the right of way is a narrow surfaced driveway. Where the driveway discontinues the right of way comes to a five bar gate. As a sign on the gate indicates to reach Alcock Tarn you should turn right once through this gate to cross a footbridge spanning Greenhead Gill and then follow the course of the gill upstream on the other side. The path follows the course of the beck for a hundred yards or so and then branches right to ascend the enclosing fellside. Eventually the path takes a level course through a fold in the fell's slopes towards a metal gate that has been converted into a stile. (¾ mile)

3 On reaching the gate/stile the object of the walk comes in to view - Alcock Tarn. The path follows the edge of the tarn. Just beyond the far end of the tarn the path branches in two. Take the right hand branch leading to a gateless gap in the wall to the right of you. Once through this gap the path begins a zig-zagged descent in to the vale. After descending some five hundred feet the path branches in two just before reaching a metal fence enclosing a plantation of conifers. (½ mile)

4 Take the left hand branch. Within some six hundred yards the path comes to a surfaced road. Here turn right. The road soon comes to a junction. This is the old Ambleside to Grasmere road. Once more turn right. The road runs downhill past Dove Cottage and across the main A591 and on in to the centre of Grasmere village. (¾ mile)

Thomas De Quincey and Dove Cottage

Whilst Dove Cottage is pre-eminently known as the home of William Wordsworth it was also the home of Thomas De Quincey from 1809 to 1820. In a footnote he added in 1856 to his most famous work, "Confessions of an English Opium Eater", he had this to say about the valley he once lived in:-

Do the Westmorland valleys turn grey headed? O reader! this is a painful memento of some of us! Thirty years ago, a gang of Vandals (nameless, I thank heaven, to me), for the sake of building a mail-coach road that never would be wanted, carried, at a cost of £3000 to the defrauded parish, a horrid causeway of sheer granite masonry, for three-quarters-of-a-mile, right through the loveliest succession of secret forest dells and shy recesses of the lake margined by unrivalled ferns....The Grasmere before and after this outrage were two different vales.

Jenkyn's Crag

Distance	3¹/₂ miles
Total feet of climbing	500 feet
Suggested time	2 hours
Starting point	Brockhole Visitors Centre (NY 392 010)
Public transport	Bus services 555 and 599 see page 36

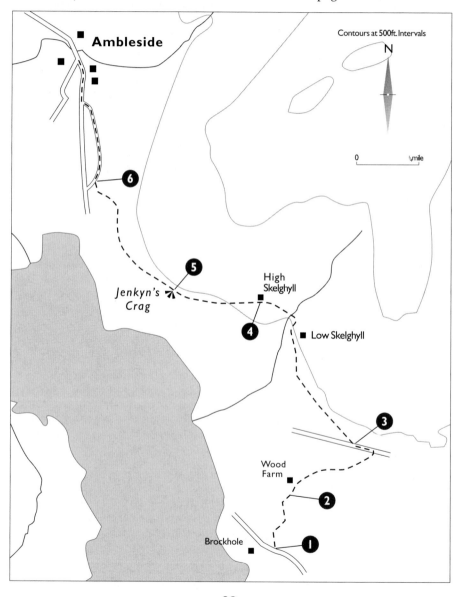

Jenkyn's Crag is a popular viewing point a little more than a mile from the centre of Ambleside. To make a visitation to this viewpoint more interesting this walk starts at Brockhole, the National Park's Visitors Centre - or at least the bus stop for it. The route thus takes in the interesting farmsteads of Low and High Skelghyll and enjoys even better, more open, views of lake Windermere than would be the case if one simply walked there and back to Jenkyn's Crag from Ambleside. There are frequent buses that enable one to get to the walk's starting point - or to return back to it if you wish to park at Brockhole car park.

1   Affixed to the bus stop for the Brockhole Visitors Centre for buses journeying south, almost opposite the entrance the centre, is a public bridleway sign for Mirk Lane, which points up an otherwise private-looking driveway for Merewood Lodge. At the entrance to the lodge the right of way swings to the right and within another fifty yards, after passing Merewood Cottages, becomes a rough trackway that eventually joins a driveway to Wood Farm, a large breeding stable. (^{1}/$_2$ mile)

2   Here turn left but where the driveway turns in to the farm press straight ahead on to a waymarked trackway - the continuation of Mirk Lane - which eventually joins a surfaced roadway. Here turn left. Some three hundred yards along this road branching off to the right is a narrow road - Skelghyll Lane. (^{1}/$_2$ mile)

3   Though there is a large sign which informs the world that Skelghyll Lane is private this prohibition applies only to motorists, cyclists and equestrians for as a less obvious signpost indicates the roadway is also a public footpath. The lane leads to High Skelghyll Farm with only one possible point of confusion on the way at Low Skelghyll, a large three storey house. Here it might seem the road terminates but it actually continues round the back of the barn that stands to the left of the house. (1 mile)

4   On reaching High Skelghyll Farm walk across the farmyard and pass through a six bar gate at the western gable end of the farm which gives access to a rough bridleway. After four hundred yards the bridleway enters Skelghyll Wood. Two hundred yards further on is to be noted a small National Trust sign bearing the words "Jenkyn's Crag" sited next to a gap in a low level stone wall on your left. Beyond the gap is a rocky mound which is Jenkyn's Crag, a much admired viewpoint. (^{1}/$_2$ mile)

5   Shortly after passing Jenkyn's Crag the bridleway commences winding its way downhill towards Ambleside. In its latter stages the bridleway becomes surfaced as it also serves as a driveway to two or three domiciles. Eventually the bridleway reaches a surfaced roadway - the Old Lake Road. (^{3}/$_4$ mile)

6   Here turn right. This older road into Ambleside parallels the more recent A591 and offers a slightly quieter way in to the town until it merges with the A591 a few hundred yards from the Market Cross. (^{1}/$_2$ mile)

Little Langdale

Distance	4 miles
Total feet of climbing	600 feet
Suggested time	2 hours
Starting point	Elterwater car park. (NY 328 047)
Public transport	Bus service 516 see page 36

As its name implies Little Langdale is a smaller, more intimate, valley compared to it's neighbour Great Langdale. It is much quieter and less frequented than its grander counterpart. This walk takes an unusual route in to the valley through some bosky glades affording on the way one of the finest views of the dale. One of the great pleasures of the valley is to be discovered soon after joining the valley road - The Three Shires Inn.

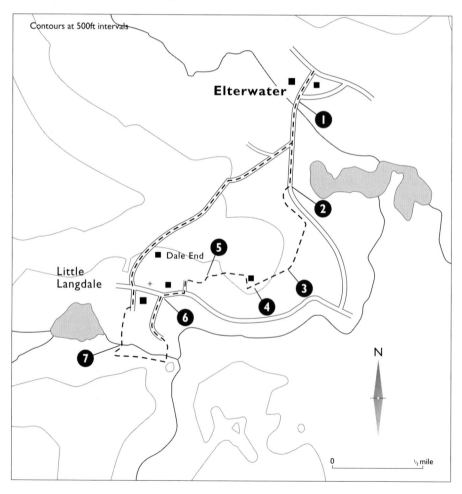

1 From the centre of Elterwater follow the road signposted as leading to Coniston and Little Langdale. Just over half a mile from the village a wooden signpost with a yellow arrow waymark indicates a public foot path entering a wood by way of stile next to a six bar gate. By the gate is a National Trust sign with the words: Fletcher Wood. (³/₄ mile)

2 Follow the trackway leading directly uphill from the gate. The track eventually comes to a gap in a stone wall which is now fenced but which has a stile affording easy passage across it. Here the track leaves the wood and follows the boundary wall of the field you have just entered arriving in the space of a hundred yards or so at a gravelled driveway. (¹/₄ mile)

3 Follow the driveway uphill. Within a few hundred yards the driveway comes to a large white gate. Pass through the gate and continue uphill. Some 100 yards further on Low Hacket, the large white house the driveway leads to, comes in view and the right of way along the driveway discontinues and instead crosses a stone stile to your left as a small sign indicates. Once over the stile turn right and follow the boundary wall and fence of Low Hacket which brings you to another stone stile. (¹/₄ mile)

4 Once over this stile continue on the same contour towards a gap in a low built wall. Once through this gap turn sharp right towards a six bar gate some thirty yards away. Passing through this gate turn left and head towards a gateway in the wall that forms the left hand boundary of the field you enter. From this gateway continue roughly down the centre of the field it gives access to. At the far end of the field is to be found a narrow metal gate. (¹/₄ mile)

5 Pass through the gate and bear left. Thirty yards away is another stone stile. Once over the stile continue down the middle of the field it gives access to to a wooden gate. After passing through this gate turn right and follow a very green trackway to Wilson Place Farm. From the farm follow the farm's access road down to the Little Langdale road. Here turn right. Within a few hundred yards, after passing - or frequenting even - the Three Shires Inn, turn left on to a lane signposted as leading to Tilberthwaite. (¹/₄ mile)

6 This lane becomes unsurfaced just before coming to the valley's river where it leads to a wooden bridge. Cross over the bridge to reach a trackway on the other side and turn right. A few hundred yards along this trackway there comes in view an unusual looking bridge spanning the river you have just crossed: Slater Bridge. Access to the bridge is via a kissing gate in the right hand enclosing wall of the trackway positioned a little way upstream from the bridge. (³/₄ mile)

7 Once over the bridge follow the distinctive steeply ascending path leading from it. The path joins an access road leading to Birk Howe Farm. Follow this access road back to the main valley road. On reaching the road turn left. Then, within the space of twenty yards, turn right on to an unsignposted lane. After passing Dale End Farm the lane becomes unsurfaced. After a further quarter of a mile the lane begins to descend and eventually reaches the road you set out on. Here turn left to return to Elterwater. (1¹/₂ miles)

Greenburn Bottom

Distance	4¹/₂ miles
Total feet of climbing	700 feet
Suggested time	2¹/₂ hours
Starting point	Grasmere (NY 328 047)
Public transport	Bus services 555 and 599 see page 36

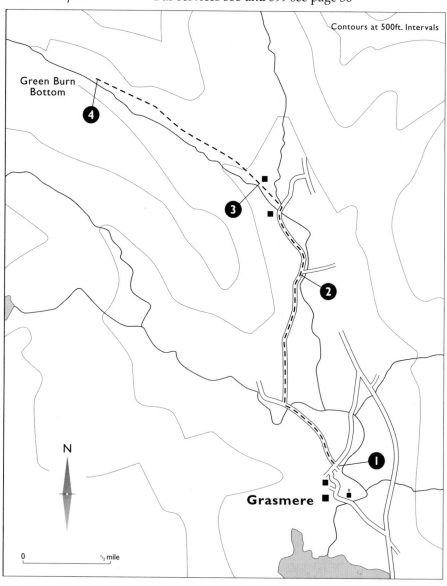

Contours at 500ft. Intervals

Green Burn Bottom

4

3

2

1

N

Grasmere

0   ¹/₂ mile

The prospect of returning to a walk's starting point the way one journeyed out is seldom an attractive option. Here, however, there is no alternative unless one takes to even higher levels. But what makes this linear - there and back - walk so worthwhile is enjoying the almost sudden experience of moving, in a few short strides, from the modern world into a world of calm and tranquillity which is the valley of Green Burn, where one might think oneself several score miles from the bustle of modern life - though it is, in truth, hardly a single mile away.

1   From Sam Read's bookshop in the centre of Grasmere walk along Easedale Road the start of which is directly opposite the bookshop. After almost half a mile distance turn right on to a lane signposted as leading to Thorney How YHA. The lane leads much further, in fact, to Low Mill Bridge where it meets a second lane. (1 mile)

2   Here turn left. Just over one quarter of a mile further on, and just after crossing over a bridge spanning Green Burn, a steep driveway leads up to the left with a sign at the entrance declaring "Private Driveway No Parking Please - Footpath Only". After crossing two cattle grids the driveway terminates at a white house called Turn Howe. ($^1/_2$ mile)

3   From here the right of way continues through a five bar gate as a rough trackway. After a climb of some four hundred and fifty feet, just before the path crosses Green Burn by way of some stepping stones, the valley opens up in to a wide spacious amphitheatre. ($^3/_4$ mile)

4   After a suitable rest return by the same way by which you arrived. (2$^1/_4$ miles)

Burns, Becks, Gills and Brooks

Burn is a common word in Scotland for stream. It derives from the Old English word *burna*. There is no reason then that we should not find it used in Lakeland but Green Burn is one of the few examples there is. Wyth Burn, just due north of Greenburn Bottom, is another but apparently this valley was originally called Wythbottom, the "burn" element only being introduced in the 17th century. There is also a Greenburn Beck in Little Langdale which would seem to be a tautology. The most common word for stream in Lakeland, of course, is beck, which comes from the Old Norse word *bekkr*. Gill is the next most common and again this derives from an Old Norse word - *gil* - which originally meant a narrow ravine but later came to mean the stream which flowed through one as well. The spelling *ghyll* seems to have been introduced into the English language by Wordsworth a born and bred Cumbrian who, strangely, never used the word beck in any of his poems. He tended instead to use the word brook which is, of course, more common to the south of England.

Easedale Tarn

Distance	4¹/₂ miles
Total feet of climbing	750 feet
Suggested time	2 1/2 hours
Starting point	Grasmere (NY 328 047)
Public transport	Bus services 555 and 599 see page 36

At four and a half miles this is a longish "short" walk. It does, however, take one in to some wild looking Lakeland scenery which is well worth making the effort to see with views of a waterfall, an isolated valley and, of course, Easedale Tarn itself. If in the 'isolated valley", Far Easedale, you happen to see walkers who are particularly burdened it is very probable they are "coast to coasters" - walkers following Wainwright's coast to coast route. If they are coming down the valley they are heading for Robin Hood's Bay on Yorkshire's North Sea coast, if walking up the valley they are heading for St. Bees Head on the west Cumbrian coast.

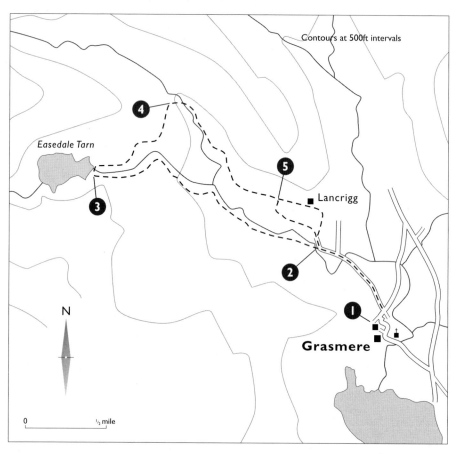

Contours at 500ft intervals

Easedale Tarn

Lancrigg

N

Grasmere

0   ¹/₂ mile

1 From Sam Read's bookshop in the centre of Grasmere walk along Easedale Road, the start of which is directly opposite the bookshop. On coming to Easedale Beck the road curves sharply to the right. Here is to be found a slate footbridge spanning the river which is signposted as being the start of a path leading to Easedale Tarn. (¹/₂ mile)

2 The path leads to a distinctive waterfall called Sourmilk Gill. Half a mile beyond the top of the waterfall the path reaches a large boulder the size, almost, of a minibus where a full view of Easedale Tarn is obtained. (1¹/₂ miles)

3 Leading away to the right from the boulder is a grassy path which leads across the outflow of the tarn and then branches in two. Follow the right hand branch which soon links on to a path which follows the downstream course of the tarn's outflow. Nearing the point where the outflow becomes the Sourmilk Gill waterfall the path veers to the left and descends in to Far Easedale. Reaching the bottom of the valley the path joins another path which follows the course of Far Easedale Gill. (³/₄ mile)

4 Here turn right and follow the valley path back towards Grasmere. The path becomes quite a broad trackway and eventually comes to a broad metal gate. (³/₄ mile)

5 Here there are two options:

The most straightforward option is to continue on the trackway. Within about a hundred yards it joins a surfaced lane. This is the same road the walk started out on. So here turn left and follow the road back to the walk's starting point. (1 mile)

Or alternatively:

Immediately after passing through the broad metal gate pass through a much smaller green metal gate to your left which gives access to a permissive path through Lancrigg Wood. The path leads to the Lancrigg Hotel, the most attractive building in the dale and one of the most congenial places in Lakeland to enjoy a pot of tea. From the hotel follow the driveway leading from it back to the road the walk began on. Here turn left and follow the road back to the walk's starting point. (1 mile)

On the 19th March 1808 at five in the evening, after attending a sale in Langdale, George Green and his wife Sarah set off over the fells to return to their home in Easedale where their six youngest children awaited their return: they never arrived. The Greens got lost in the snow and mist and darkness of nightfall. Seemingly after several hours of disorientated wandering they fell to their deaths. Their bodies were discovered four days later only a quarter of a mile from the nearest dwelling. A fund was established by the people of Grasmere, including the Wordsworths, to provide for their orphaned offspring.

Public Transport

The starting point of all the walks in this guide can be reached using public transport. There are five relevant bus services:-

Grasmere - Ambleside - Brockhole - Services 555 and 599

Both these services follow the A591. The 555 operates all year round between Keswick and Lancaster. The 599 is seasonal and operates between Grasmere and Bowness or Kendal.

Ambleside - Skelwith Bridge - Elterwater - Dungeon Ghyll -Service 516

The 516 is given the name Langdale Rambler as it operates from Ambleside to Dungeon Ghyll at the head of the Langdale valley. At the time of writing it doesn't do a lot of rambling - there are only six runs a day and on weekdays the last bus to ramble back to Ambleside is back by two minutes past five!

Skelwith Bridge to Ambleside - Service 506

This is known as the Coniston Rambler and does even less rambling than the Langdale Rambler - four times a day and only thrice on Sunday, and is seasonal only.

Windermere to Troutbeck - Service 108A

This service runs from Bowness to Glenridding. It is a very limited service and only operates seasonally and for most of that period for weekends only.

Timetables for all the above services are usually well displayed at the relevant bus stops. In addition for some years now Stagecoach have produced a very useful timetable brochure which is obtainable at all information centres and usually on all their buses as well from April to October. For phone enquiries telephone 0870 608 2 608.

Buses are quite expensive in the Lake District there are, though, four day passes which can cut the cost of having to rely on them quite considerably.

March, 2002

Is iad seo na focail dheireanacha sa leabhar!